Original title:
The Winter Path

Author: Kätriin Kaldaru
ISBN HARDBACK: 978-9916-79-354-1
ISBN PAPERBACK: 978-9916-79-355-8
ISBN EBOOK: 978-9916-79-356-5

Dreams on a Chilling Breeze

Whispers of night on frosty air,
Chasing starlight, without a care.
Hopes drift softly, like feathers fall,
In the silence, we hear the call.

Moonlit paths lead to the unknown,
Where shadows dance and dreams have grown.
In every breath, the magic sings,
Along the way, the heart finds wings.

Harbor of Frosted Whispers

Nestled beneath the winter's breath,
Silent secrets held close to death.
In the harbor where echoes blend,
Frosted whispers, hearts will mend.

Gentle tides caress the shore,
Memories linger, wanting more.
Lost in time, the stories weave,
Of love and loss, we still believe.

Frozen Footprints in Twilight

Shadows stretch beneath the dusk,
Footsteps etched in twilight's husk.
Moments captured, cold as ice,
In silence, we pay the price.

Every print tells a tale of old,
Of dreams once bright, now icy cold.
Through emerald forests, we wander on,
In pursuit of the fading dawn.

Shimmering Silence of Snow

Snowflakes dance in whispered light,
Covering the world in white.
Every flake a song of peace,
In their descent, our worries cease.

Softly falling, the moments weave,
In shimmering silence, hearts believe.
Nature's quilt, a gentle embrace,
In winter's glow, we find our place.

A Tread of Stillness Through Snowfall

In the hush of winter's breath,
Footsteps soft as dreams,
Blankets white kiss the earth,
Whispers fade in gleams.

Trees wear coats of crystal lace,
Branches bow with grace,
Silent echoes fill the space,
Time slows its pace.

Shadows dance in fading light,
Figures move so slow,
Every flake a fleeting sight,
In this world of snow.

Through the woods where silence reigns,
Stillness hugs the night,
Calm descends on gentle plains,
Bathed in soft moonlight.

Nature breathes, a peaceful sigh,
Heartbeats blend in tune,
In this moment, no goodbye,
Wrapped in winter’s rune.

Flakes Falling Like Soft Whispers

Flakes drift down from clouds above,
Like secrets shared with the night,
Each one carries a tale of love,
Glowing soft in pale moonlight.

A hush descends on frozen streams,
Silent stories, they unfold,
Wrapped within winter's dreams,
Tales of warmth in the cold.

Frosty air carries a tune,
Nature’s symphony plays soft,
As flakes flutter down like a boon,
In the silence, they waft.

Softly, they layer the ground,
A white quilt quietly laid,
In this peaceful light, we're found,
As new memories are made.

Underneath the starlit sky,
Every flake is a sigh,
Whispers echo, shy and spry,
As time glides quietly by.

The Stillness After the Storm

The winds have ceased, a hush in the air,
Nature holds its breath, with a tranquil glare.
Branches bowed low, kissed by the rain,
Earth reclaims peace, where chaos had lain.

Clouds drift away, unveiling the blue,
Sunlight breaks through, warm and anew.
Puddles reflect, a world glimmers bright,
In the stillness found, hearts feel the light.

Paths Woven in Whispering Snow

Footprints imprint on the glistening snow,
Silent stories of where we shall go.
Whispers of winter dance through the trees,
Softly they sing with an icy breeze.

Each flake a secret, a tale to be spun,
With laughter and joy as bright as the sun.
Paths intertwine like the threads of our fate,
In the hush of the snow, we find love's gate.

Trading Warmth for Winter Wonder

Cozy fires glow, but the heart longs to roam,
Through fields draped in white, we find a new home.
Trading our warmth for the beauty outside,
Where snowflakes twirl like a jubilant ride.

Bundled in layers, we venture out bright,
Sleds racing down hills, laughter takes flight.
Each moment a treasure, a joy to recall,
In winter's embrace, we find warmth in all.

Heartbeats Beneath the Ice

Beneath the ice, where silence does dwell,
Lies the rhythm of life, a secret to tell.
Pulsing softly, in shadows it waits,
The heartbeat of earth in the frost that sedates.

Under the surface, dreams begin to grow,
In the cold embrace, life's wonders still flow.
Awaken the still, let the thaw take its course,
For love endures, a never-ending force.

Captured by the Chill

The air is sharp, the silence speaks,
Winter's grip, its icy peaks.
Every breath, a misty plume,
Nature wraps us in its gloom.

Footprints crunch on frosted ground,
In this stillness, peace is found.
Branches bare, the sky so gray,
Captured by the chill of day.

Frosted windows, candles glow,
Whispers soft, the fire's flow.
Time slows down, a breath in time,
Wrapped in warmth, so safe, sublime.

Frozen lakes, reflections still,
Hearts embrace the winter's thrill.
As the world sleeps beneath white,
There's magic hidden in the night.

Serenity Amongst the Snowdrifts

Snowflakes dance, a quiet song,
In this moment, we belong.
Blankets white on quiet lands,
Nature rests in gentle hands.

Silence sings through every tree,
Whispers of serenity.
In the shadows, soft and light,
Snowdrifts capture pure delight.

Footsteps lead to tranquil views,
Footprints trace where peace imbues.
Hearts awakened by the glow,
Find our solace deep in snow.

Each breath taken, calm and slow,
In this world, the softest flow.
Serene heart, the winter's grace,
Lingers here, a warm embrace.

Voices of the Winter Woods

In the woods, the whispers call,
Echoes bounce from tree to wall.
Branches rustle, shadows weave,
Tales of winter, who would believe?

Crisp and clear, the air defines,
Breath of frost on ancient pines.
Echoes carried on the breeze,
Voices mingle through the trees.

Nature speaks in hushed tones,
Every rustle, every moan.
From the thickets, secrets bloom,
Winter hides its quiet doom.

Every step, a story told,
In this realm, the air turns cold.
Listen close, the whispers play,
Voices of the woods will stay.

Frosty Breath of the Trees

Trees stand tall, clad in white,
In stillness, they glow bright.
Frosty breath, a gentle sigh,
Nature's canvas, pure and high.

From the branches, icicles hang,
Winter's song, a silent clang.
Every leaf, a crystal shard,
A frozen beauty, silent guard.

Underneath the snow's embrace,
Life still dreams, in hidden space.
Roots entwined in frost's tight grip,
Awaiting spring's soft, warm trip.

The breath of trees holds stories deep,
Secrets whispered, dreams to keep.
In frosty air, their spirits cling,
The cold might wait, but hope will spring.

Coffee and Cold Beneath the Pines

Morning mist hugs the earth,
A cup warms my hands,
Whispers in the crisp air,
Pine needles make soft bands.

Steam rises toward the sky,
Promises of the sun,
Each sip holds a memory,
Of trails yet to run.

Frosted branches glisten bright,
Nature’s calm embrace,
In this serene stillness,
I find my sacred place.

Beneath towering giants,
I let the world still,
With coffee as my anchor,
And dreams that softly spill.

The day unfurls like petals,
With adventures at hand,
But here in quiet moments,
I learn to understand.

Stars Alight on Snowy Nights

A blanket of pure silence,
Covers the sleeping land,
Stars like diamonds scattered,
Across a sky so grand.

The moon peeks through the trees,
Casting shadows soft and light,
While the world curls in slumber,
Wrapped in the arms of night.

Snowflakes dance like whispers,
Falling with gentle grace,
Each one a fleeting moment,
In winter's cold embrace.

The air is crisp and clear,
With magic in each breath,
Underneath the starry quilt,
Life finds beauty in depth.

I stroll through this wonder,
My heart sings with delight,
For in nature’s stillness,
The stars alight the night.

Tranquil Steps in a Silver World

The world wrapped in silver,
Each branch adorned with frost,
Every step is a whisper,
A moment never lost.

The path winds like a river,
Through pine and open glade,
Where shadows merge with light,
In this serene cascade.

Gentle crunch beneath my feet,
Echoes in the still,
A song of nature's heartbeat,
In perfect winter's chill.

Breath forms clouds in the air,
As the sun begins to rise,
Illuminating the world,
With hues of soft surprise.

Each moment feels like magic,
As I wander with delight,
In a tranquil silver world,
Where dreams take gentle flight.

The Dance of Ice and Silence

The world wrapped in satin,
Ice glistens in the dawn,
Each angle holds a secret,
In beauty's quiet yawn.

Shadows stretch across the snow,
Soft whispers fill the air,
In the dance of ice and silence,
Magic dwells everywhere.

Branches bow with heavy frost,
A tapestry so fine,
As the stillness wraps around,
Each moment is divine.

Nature’s breath is muted,
A peaceful, rhythmic sound,
Where time slows and lingers,
And serenity is found.

I watch the world in silence,
With wonder etched in heart,
For in this icy ballet,
I glimpse a work of art.

The Tranquility of Snow-laden Branches

Silent whispers fill the night,
Branches bow with gentle grace.
Snowflakes dance in soft moonlight,
Nature's peace in every space.

Quiet thoughts drift on the breeze,
Blanketing the earth below.
Time stands still beneath the trees,
A world wrapped in velvet snow.

Frozen dreams in crystalline forms,
Softened edges round each limb.
Holding still the wildest storms,
A moment caught, both brief and dim.

In the hush, the heart can hear,
Voices of the winter's charm.
Snow-laden branches, crystal clear,
Embrace the calm with quiet arms.

A tapestry of glimmering white,
Sealing secrets in their shroud.
In the stillness, pure delight,
Nature whispers; soft, unbowed.

Hushed Conversations with the Cold

In the quiet of the night,
Frosty breath on window panes.
Whispers blend with silver light,
Nature speaks in gentle strains.

Shadows dance upon the floor,
Echoes of a world outside.
Winter's chill, a soft encore,
Inviting warmth that can’t abide.

Each sigh wraps around the heart,
Tender meetings in the frost.
In this realm, we play our part,
Finding solace in the lost.

Moments linger, fleeting fast,
Caught between the warm and chill.
Hushed conversations that can last,
In the stillness, time stands still.

Life flows gently, soft and slow,
In this quiet, we confide.
Hushed dialogues with the cold,
Breathe in peace, let worries slide.

Trail of Secrets in White Draperies

Footprints lead through fields of white,
Stories buried 'neath the glow.
Each step whispers of delight,
In the silence, secrets flow.

The earth wrapped in softest hush,
Draped in layers, smooth and sleek.
Time moves slow, a gentle rush,
In this place, the heart can speak.

Snowflakes swirl like whispered dreams,
Painting tales on branches bare.
In the quiet, nothing seems,
Lost in wonder, floating air.

Follow paths where no one treads,
Map the silence, hear its song.
Wrapped in warmth, the spirit spreads,
Finding where the heart belongs.

In the drapery of snow,
Each moment spun, a story told.
Follow slowly where dreams go,
In white, a treasure to behold.

Etching Stories in Frosty Air

Breath of winter shapes the scene,
Frosty paintings on the glass.
Every sigh, a fleeting sheen,
Moments caught that dare to pass.

In the stillness, tales emerge,
Written soft in icy breath.
Nature's hand begins to urge,
Stories shared beyond the death.

Laughter bounces through the cold,
Echoes dance beneath the stars.
In the frost, great truths unfold,
Awakening forgotten scars.

Each whisper clings to night’s embrace,
Veils of frost on every face.
Echoes linger, time can trace,
Life’s adventures we must chase.

Through the twilight, paths anew,
Etched in air, like dreams we share.
In the freeze, we start to view,
The tales born in the frosty air.

Frozen Thorns and Barren Boughs

In winter's clutch, the thorns ensnared,
Barren boughs reach, their beauty impaired.
Silent whispers of a season's chill,
Nature sleeps, holding time still.

Shadows dance on the frosty ground,
A symphony of silence wraps around.
Each breath a mist, a ghostly thread,
Echoes of life remain softly said.

Beneath the frost, a story untold,
Of dreams and warmth in the night's cold hold.
Frozen thorns across the landscape lie,
Waiting for spring beneath the gray sky.

The wind, it sighs through the vacant trees,
In their starkness, a haunting breeze.
Barren moments stretch like daylight dreams,
In the chill, the heart quietly gleams.

Reflections in a Crystal Pool

Beneath the sky, a pool so bright,
Holds the whisper of the fading light.
Mirrored stillness, a tranquil embrace,
Where water captures nature's grace.

Clouds drift above, painting the scene,
In the crystal depths, colors glean.
Soft ripples break the perfect view,
Each wave a song that feels so new.

Ducks glide gently, a ballet bold,
In reflected beauty, stories unfold.
The sun dips low, a golden hue,
Kissing the water, a farewell true.

Surrounded by reeds, tall and proud,
Nature's whispers, soft yet loud.
In this haven, time stands still,
Gravity lost in the gentle thrill.

A Symphony of Cold and Calm

Snowflakes flutter, a delicate dance,
Whispering tales of a winter's chance.
Beneath the frost, a world asleep,
In the hush, secrets is ours to keep.

Pines stand tall, cloaked in white,
Guardians of silence in the fading light.
The air crisp, a refreshing bite,
Framed in stillness, a tranquil sight.

A distant echo of an owl's call,
The night embraces, wraps us all.
In shadows cast by the moon's glow,
The heart whispers what the stars know.

Footprints trace where the wild things roam,
In this winter landscape, we find our home.
A symphony plays in the still of the night,
In every silence, the world's pure light.

The Blanketed Earth

A gentle hush falls over the land,
Where snowflakes gather, soft as sand.
The earth is blanketed, pure and white,
A canvas of calm in the fading light.

Fields lie dormant, quiet and deep,
In winter's embrace, nature's sleep.
Every tree draped in a frosty shroud,
A silent beauty, silent and proud.

Footsteps crunch on the frozen ground,
Each step a miracle, each sound profound.
In this stillness, hearts find their song,
In the blanket of snow, we all belong.

The season's breath whispers soft and low,
Comforting warmth in the midst of snow.
As we wander through this winter's breath,
We find life's pulse, even in death.

When the World Turns White

Snowflakes dance in winter's breath,
Covering earth with gentle dress.
Every tree and every lane,
Transforming all with quiet gain.

Footsteps crunch on frozen trails,
Whispers float through icy gales.
The world is hushed, a tranquil scene,
Nature wrapped in silver sheen.

Children laugh, their cheeks aglow,
Building dreams in purest snow.
A snowman smiles, a scarf so bright,
Embodying joy in the faded light.

Quiet nights with stars so near,
Frosty air brings warmth and cheer.
Underneath a moonlit sky,
All worries drift and gently fly.

In this white, we pause and stare,
Breathe in peace, a life laid bare.
The world transforms, a canvas white,
In winter's grip, everything feels right.

Lanterns in the Snowfall

Tiny lights in falling snow,
Glisten softly, warm and glow.
Hanging high or placed down low,
Guiding hearts where dreams can flow.

Children point and laugh with glee,
At lanterns dancing, wild and free.
Each flicker tells a tender tale,
Of winter nights and whispering trails.

Footsteps echo on the street,
In the hush, their pulse beats sweet.
Snowflakes twirl in the cool night air,
As lanterns sway without a care.

Glistening paths lead far and wide,
Each glowing orb a gentle guide.
In the night, they softly gleam,
Illuminating every dream.

Let the warmth of light unfold,
In winter's grasp, through days so cold.
Lanterns in the snowfall bright,
Bring us hope and pure delight.

Beneath the Weight of Silence

Frost lays heavy on the ground,
In the stillness, peace is found.
Each breath rises, a cloud of white,
Beneath the weight of calm delight.

Time stands still, the world asleep,
Promises held in silence deep.
Echoes fade, just a whisper's tone,
In this haven, we are alone.

Moonlight dances on the frost,
In the quiet, nothing's lost.
Every star a story told,
In this silence, dreams unfold.

Whispers linger on the breeze,
Carrying hope through barren trees.
Within this weight, we find our grace,
In the stillness, we embrace.

Beneath the weight of endless night,
We search for comfort, warmth, and light.
In silence vast, we start to know,
The beauty in the falling snow.

Glimmering Stars on the Frigid Ground

Stars shine brightly in the night,
Reflecting on the blankets white.
Each glimmer holds a cosmic spark,
Illuminating paths through dark.

The ground below, a frosted sheet,
Wears a dress both soft and neat.
Whispers float as cool winds blow,
In this magic, time moves slow.

As creatures nest and shadows creep,
The world wraps close in icy sleep.
Mirrored starlight guides the way,
In the stillness of the day.

Dreams entwined with winter's chill,
Hearts beat softly, time stands still.
Glimmering stars, the night's embrace,
Hold the promise of a warm grace.

In this landscape, pure and true,
Nature sings a song anew.
Glimmering stars on the frigid ground,
In their beauty, love is found.

The Hushed Lullaby of Cold

In the night, whispers softly,
Blankets of white enfold the earth.
Stars gaze down, their light dimmed,
As winter sings its gentle tune.

Frosted trees stand in silence,
Swaying like dancers lost in dreams.
Breath forms clouds in the stillness,
Nature wrapped in a shivering sigh.

Moonlight spills like silver threads,
On the canvas of darkened skies.
Each flake tells a story,
Of warmth found in cold embrace.

Hushed lullabies weave through branches,
Crickets rest, their songs silenced.
A world hushed under frosty whispers,
Carried away in the night air.

In this quiet, peace settles deep,
A melody of frost and dreams.
For in the cold, comfort blossoms,
Holding us close 'til the dawn breaks.

A Tapestry of Snow and Stillness

Threaded white across the ground,
A tapestry woven of dreams.
Each flake a whisper of silence,
Embracing the world in stillness.

Trees wear coats of crystal beauty,
Branches burdened with purest grace.
Beneath the weight, they perfectly bow,
Nature adorned in winter's charm.

Footsteps fade into the white,
Stories left behind in the frost.
Echoes linger in the cold night,
Where whispers of the past reside.

With each breath, the air shimmers,
Frozen lace of frost encircles.
Time pauses in this sacred realm,
A moment caught between the worlds.

In the quiet, the heart stirs gently,
Drifting with the wind's soft caress.
Wrapped in this beauty, we're alive,
In a tapestry of snow and calm.

Footprints in the Soft Snow

Fresh snow blankets the waking ground,
A canvas waiting for a trace.
Each step leaves a story behind,
Footprints dance in the winter's grace.

Whispers of secrets held in silence,
With every mark, a tale unfolds.
The soft crunch beneath each movement,
A rhythm echoing in the cold.

Curves and lines weave through the drifts,
A path of journeys both past and new.
Like echoes of laughter in the air,
Memories held in the pale view.

As twilight wraps the world in shadows,
Footprints shimmer, kissed by the moon.
A testament to share what was,
In this soft realm where dreams are strewn.

With every step, let joy be known,
In this snowy embrace, we're home.
Footprints lead us back to warmth,
As whispers of winter softly roam.

Embrace of the Chilling Air

Bitter winds weave through the trees,
An embrace colder than twilight.
Nature shivers, yet breathes deeply,
In the chill, there’s a pure delight.

Frosty kisses paint the window,
Delicate patterns like lace unfurled.
The air crackles with crisp magic,
Every breath a glimpse of the world.

Through stillness, the heart finds solace,
Wrapped warmly in winter's hold.
A place where dreams linger softly,
In the embrace of the chilling cold.

Echoed in whispers of icy nights,
The beauty lies in stark contrast.
For in the depths of freezing breath,
We discover warmth that holds steadfast.

So let the chill paint on the canvas,
Woven memories of ice and frost.
In each gust, the heartbeat beckons,
Finding love in what feels lost.

Sledding down Memory Lane

Snowflakes swirl in the chilly breeze,
Laughter echoes through the tall, bare trees.
Sleds glide fast, carving out tracks,
Memories made, no looking back.

Each push down feels like a dream,
Frosty faces aglow with gleam.
Whispers of joy in the winter air,
Moments like these, nothing can compare.

Crisp air bites, but spirits soar,
Bundled up, we crave for more.
A rush of thrill with each new bend,
We ride together, hearts to mend.

In patches where the sunlight fades,
Laughter lingers in fleeting glades.
With every run, a story told,
Adventures shared, forever bold.

As twilight falls, we gather near,
Exchanging tales, laughter sincere.
Forever etched in heart and mind,
Sledding down, love intertwined.

Shards of Light in a Brilliant White

Sunrise paints the world anew,
A canvas stretched in radiant hue.
Shards of light cut through the frost,
In this wonderland, we find what's lost.

Glittering snow like diamonds glow,
Frost drapes over the fields below.
Every glance, a sparkling delight,
In the embrace of a brilliant white.

Footprints lead us where we tread,
In the silence, all fears shed.
Moments frozen in time's embrace,
An icy sparkle, a tranquil space.

Nature's quiet, a soothing balm,
In the stillness, we feel so calm.
Each breath we take, crisp and clear,
We find our solace, far from fear.

In this realm where dreams ignite,
We dance beneath the soft twilight.
Shards of light in white fields bloom,
Filling our hearts, dispelling gloom.

Whispers of the Frostbitten Air

Whispers carried on crisp, cold winds,
Tales of winter where silence begins.
Frostbitten air bites at our skin,
But in its chill, warmth lies within.

Pine trees stand like sentinels tall,
Guardians of secrets, they hear our call.
Footsteps crunch on a blanket of white,
We wander through wonders, hearts full of light.

Snowflakes dance in the muted glow,
A soft, gentle hush, a comforting show.
Wrapped in layers, we share our dreams,
In this season where magic redeems.

Moments freeze as time passes slow,
Each breath a mist, in the evening's flow.
Whispers of hope in the frosty air,
Remind us again how much we care.

As shadows stretch and daylight fades,
We find warmth in these snowy glades.
Whispers of peace as stars appear,
Frostbitten air brings us near.

Solace in Icy Shadows

In the depths of a winter’s night,
We seek solace in shadows of white.
Dancing lights in the cool, still air,
Embracing the calm, no room for care.

Snow blankets the earth in muted grace,
A soft embrace, a tranquil space.
Our laughter mingles with the night,
In icy shadows, our hearts take flight.

Each flake falls like a whispered sigh,
Nature's lullaby beneath the starry sky.
Finding comfort in the frosty chill,
With every heartbeat, the world stands still.

The moon glows bright, a guiding hand,
Illuminating this enchanted land.
Through the stillness, our souls unwind,
In icy shadows, peace we find.

Together we wander, side by side,
In these moments, we won’t hide.
Solace speaks, as the night unfolds,
In chilly embrace, warmth never grows old.

A Canvas of Snow and Shadows

Snowflakes fall like whispers,
Covering the world in white.
Shadows dance beneath the trees,
Guided by the soft moonlight.

Each footprint tells a story,
Of journeys made in silent night.
The air is crisp and fleeting,
A canvas pure and bright.

Branches draped in silver threads,
Sway gently in the breeze.
Nature's art, a tranquil sight,
Whispers through the frozen leaves.

Stars peek through the twilight hues,
Painting dreams across the sky.
In this serene, enchanted place,
Hearts and spirits seem to fly.

As dawn breaks the quiet spell,
Colors blend and come alive.
The canvas of snow and shadows,
Awakens, dreams begin to thrive.

The Frost's Gentle Caress

Morning light gleams on the grass,
A blanket of frost, soft and clear.
Each blade wears a sparkling crown,
Nature's touch, both cold and dear.

The world rests in a shimmering glow,
As silence wraps the waking land.
Frost’s caress, a tender hold,
Embracing all with delicate hands.

Trees stand proud, dressed in white,
Their branches bow with icy grace.
Whispers of winter linger low,
In this still and frozen space.

Birds flit by in joyous flight,
Seeking seeds where warmth does dwell.
The sun breaks through, a golden beam,
Casting magic, weaving spells.

In every breath, the chill remains,
Yet hearts stay warm beneath this sky.
The frost’s gentle caress, we cherish,
In its quiet beauty, we sigh.

Chasing Dreams Amidst the Chill

In the cold, our laughter rings,
As snowflakes fall, twirling down.
We chase the dreams that winter brings,
In a world of white and brown.

Boundless fields, our playground vast,
Snowmen rise, our hopes align.
Each moment fleeting, memories cast,
In the chill, our spirits shine.

Sleds racing fast down hills of white,
Joyful shouts break through the frost.
Chasing dreams, we take to flight,
No adventure feels like a loss.

With every breath, our warmth ignites,
Against the chill, we stand as one.
In this wonderland of snowy sights,
Our hearts beat strong beneath the sun.

As twilight falls, the stars awake,
Adventures linger on the breeze.
Chasing dreams, we never break,
Together, we find moments of peace.

Secrets Hidden Under Frosted Skies

Beneath the frost, whispers dwell,
Hidden secrets kept in snow.
Each flake a story, yet to tell,
In winter's hold, where mysteries grow.

Trees wear crowns of icy lace,
Their shadows stretch as daylight fades.
The world transforms, a still embrace,
While night descends, and silence invades.

Footsteps crunch on hidden paths,
Leading to where few have roamed.
Frosted breath and gentle laughs,
In this realm, we feel at home.

Stars above like diamonds shine,
Guardians of the dreams we chase.
Secrets nestled in the pine,
In the dark, we find our place.

As dawn breaks with golden hue,
The frost melts and stories rise.
Secrets hidden, now in view,
Underneath these frosted skies.

Between Darkness and Light in February

In the chill of a fading dusk,
Shadows dance and softly hush.
The world, wrapped in cold embrace,
Awaits the dawn's warm, tender grace.

Whispers of hope in the night air,
Twinkle of stars, a gentle prayer.
Beneath a blanket, deep and vast,
The heart beats slow; the moment lasts.

Frost-kissed branches, silver threads,
Glistening dreams where silence spreads.
A flicker breaks the darkened sky,
As February bids the shadows goodbye.

The snowflakes fall, a muted sigh,
Painting paths, as time drifts by.
Between shadows and hopeful light,
Lives the promise of morning bright.

The moon watches with a tender gaze,
Guiding souls through twilight's maze.
In this space where dreams take flight,
We find our way, between dark and light.

The Haunting Beauty of Frozen Stillness

In frozen fields where silence clings,
A crystal hush, the world still sings.
The beauty wrapped in winter's frost,
Echoes of warmth, a dream embossed.

Bare branches reach for skies of gray,
Touching whispers of a brighter day.
Ghostly shapes in the moon's light,
A haunting dance of day and night.

Footsteps muffled in the snow,
Silent secrets only they know.
Each flake a memory, caught in time,
A gentle reminder, so sublime.

The wind weaves tales of yesteryear,
In every breath, a voice so clear.
Frozen stillness, a tranquil art,
Capturing moments that touch the heart.

In this realm where shadows blend,
Beauty thrives, yet seems to bend.
The haunting echoes, soft and bright,
Invite us closer, to the night.

Frostbitten Dreams Under Starry Skies

Beneath the stars, a frigid dream,
Whispers float on a silver stream.
The night, a canvas of endless space,
Awakens thoughts with a gentle grace.

Frostbitten air, crisp and clear,
Echoes of laughter linger near.
Stars sprinkle magic across the dark,
Each twinkle brings a hopeful spark.

The world lies hushed in slumber deep,
As frost-kissed secrets start to seep.
Awakening dreams in the still of night,
Boundless journeys take off in flight.

A blanket of stars, a shimmering sea,
Inviting hearts to drift and be free.
In the cold, we find warmth inside,
In frostbitten dreams, hopes abide.

Wrapped in night's gentle embrace,
We discover stillness, a sacred space.
Under the stars, where dreams ignite,
Frostbitten visions blur the line of sight.

Echoes of Solitude in the White Abyss

In the depths of a winter's breath,
Lies a silence that speaks of death.
The white abyss, a canvas bare,
Holds the echoes of a wandering prayer.

Footprints lost in the endless sea,
Carved by whispers of who used to be.
In solitude's hold, we find our way,
As shadows stretch to greet the day.

The frosty wind carries a sigh,
A melody of days gone by.
In the hush of snow, a soft refrain,
Resounds with the beauty of joy and pain.

Desolation wrapped in a cloak of white,
Gives birth to dreams in the heart of night.
The echoes linger, softly profound,
In the white abyss, the lost are found.

Each flake that falls, a memory born,
Touching the soul, gently worn.
In solitude's dance, we rise and fall,
Echoes of life, the winter's call.

A Breath Between Seasons of Ice

Frosted winds softly sigh,
Whispers of warmth through the pines.
A fleeting hope flickers by,
As sunlight dances, then resigns.

Nature holds its breath anew,
Waiting for the thaw's embrace.
In the stillness, life's breakthrough,
The pulse of spring finds its place.

Branches drip with crystal tears,
A symphony of melting day.
Each moment feeds the quiet fears,
Of winter's grip, of soft decay.

Yet, in this pause, heartbeats grow,
The earth, a canvas, faintly speaks.
From the depth, the green will show,
Renewal springs from hidden peaks.

A breath between the chill and bloom,
In twilight where the seasons shift.
Hope stirs gently, dispelling gloom,
As life prepares its precious gift.

Underneath a Cloak of White

Beneath the hush of drifting snow,
Silent dreams in the stillness grow.
A blanket softens every sound,
In this peace, solace is found.

Footprints lead through the quiet night,
Guided by soft, ethereal light.
Stars peek down through swirling mist,
Each heartbeat wrapped in winter's tryst.

Branches bare are cloaked in white,
Nature's hush, a tranquil sight.
A world transformed, serene and bright,
Underneath this spellbound night.

In the distance, whispers call,
Echoes soft, like snowflakes fall.
Here in dreams, we drift and sway,
A moment held, a winter's play.

Underneath this cloak, we find,
The pulse of peace, the heart's unwind.
Each flake a wish, each flurry a hope,
In the delicate dance, we learn to cope.

Pathways Through the Pale Expanse

Winding trails through snow-dusted trees,
Each step whispers secrets with ease.
Footfalls crunch on this frozen ground,
In silence, the heart's song is found.

Pine boughs bow with a heavy load,
Nature's breath where shadows strode.
The sky stretches in shades of gray,
Painting dreams that drift and sway.

A frozen lake reflects the sky,
Mirrored moments where echoes lie.
Winds carry tales of times undone,
Pathways forged where the rivers run.

With each turning turn, new sights unfold,
In crisp air, winter's wonders told.
Through the pale expanse, we roam,
Finding in stillness, a way back home.

Every pathway leads to the heart,
A journey begun is a brand new start.
In nature's art, we see the truth,
Embracing the wonder of wintertime youth.

Dreams Adrift in Snowy Whispers

In the hush of snowy realms,
Dreams adrift on ethereal helms.
Each whisper carries a tender tale,
Floating softly on the winter gale.

Blanketed hopes wrapped tight in white,
Captured moments of soft twilight.
Dance of shadows, flicker, and glide,
In the stillness, our fears subside.

Beneath the stars, the world seems small,
Crystalline magic where nightbirds call.
Every flake a wish upon the breeze,
In the silent depths, hearts find their ease.

Cascading thoughts like snowflakes fall,
In the chill, we find warmth in the thrall.
Dreams entwined in a winter's spell,
Stories told in a soft, icy shell.

Adrift we sail on whispers' sigh,
Where love and silence softly lie.
In dreams woven with glistening threads,
A tapestry where hope gently spreads.

Fragments of Frost on My Skin

A whisper of chill in the air,
Tiny crystals land with care.
Each touch a story, ice-kissed dreams,
Nature's artistry, so it seems.

The sun peeks shy through the trees,
Glistening bright, a gentle tease.
In delicate patterns, life unfolds,
Tales of magic, softly told.

Bare branches sway, the cold winds sigh,
Seeking warmth beneath the sky.
Layers of frost cloak ground and stone,
In this moment, I am not alone.

The world turns white, serene and still,
Nature’s silence, a heart to fill.
Each breath is visible, a sigh of grace,
In the heart of winter, I find my place.

Fragments of peace, a frozen bliss,
Crystals shimmer with winter's kiss.
In the chill, I find my glow,
Fragments of frost, my spirit in tow.

The Quiet Dance of Falling Snow

Softly it lands, a gentle plight,
Veils of white in the fading light.
Each flake unique, a fleeting art,
Whispers of winter, straight to the heart.

Twirling and swirling, a ballet unseen,
Bringing a hush to each passing scene.
Gravity's grip in delicate grace,
Layers of snow, a soft embrace.

Footprints vanish, the ground a new page,
Nature writes stories, timeless as sage.
In the stillness, a world reborn,
In the quiet, a soft, new dawn.

Each flake a promise, a wish to be,
Carried on winds, wild and free.
The quiet dance weaves dreams in the air,
Magic of winter, a moment so rare.

Together they fall, in peaceful descent,
Nature's lullaby, pure and gentle,
In this silent performance, beauty glows,
The quiet dance of falling snow.

Serenity on a Frozen Path

A path laid bare, draped in white,
Each step whispers, calm and light.
In frozen silence, worries melt,
Moments of clarity, deeply felt.

Frosty edges encircle my view,
Soft light dances, the day feels new.
Beneath the sky, such peace I find,
Serenity whispers, gently entwined.

Pine trees stand tall, cloaked in snow,
Their stillness teaches what hearts can know.
Every breath, a fleeting breath,
In this stillness, I find my depth.

Tracks behind me tell stories of old,
Of journeys taken, brave and bold.
With each new step, I’m drawn to the light,
Walking on dreams through the endless white.

Serenity beckons, on this frozen path,
Guiding my spirit, calming my wrath.
In moments of stillness, I truly see,
Nature's reflection, the essence of me.

Winter's Silent Embrace

In shadows of twilight, the world stands still,
Wrapped in a blanket of winter’s chill.
Silent moments, the heartbeats slow,
In winter's grasp, the quiet flows.

Breath fogs in the crisp, clear air,
Each exhale a whisper, tender and rare.
A dance of stillness in falling night,
Winter holds close, a gentle light.

Stars peek down from their velvet shroud,
Witnessing dreams in the softest crowd.
Every crystal sparkles, each shadow holds,
Stories of winter, quiet and bold.

A hug from nature, vast and wide,
In frozen moments, I take my ride.
Each heartbeat echoes, lost in the snow,
Wrapped in the magic, the softest glow.

Winter's embrace, a soothing balm,
Whispers of peace, a perfect calm.
In the still of the night, my spirit flies,
In winter's silent arms, my heart always lies.

Crystal Dreams Unfold

In twilight's breath, the colors blend,
Soft whispers call, like old friends send.
Crystal visions, shimmer bright,
Magic dances in the night.

A gentle breeze, the shadows play,
Guiding thoughts, as night meets day.
Through silken paths, we walk on air,
In dreams of hope, we lose all care.

Starlit dreams, a canvas wide,
Where wishes bloom, and fears subside.
Each spark a tale, a wish anew,
In crystal realms, we dare pursue.

With open hearts, we take a chance,
Unraveled threads in fate's own dance.
As dawn approaches, softly glows,
Our crystal dreams, a bright encore.

Together we rise, hand in hand,
In sparkles strewn across the land.
What once was murk, is clear and bold,
In the realm where dreams unfold.

Silent Journey Through the Frost

Amidst the woods, the silence reigns,
Where frosty breath is all that remains.
Footsteps muffled, the world so still,
A journey begun, on winter's hill.

Each flake descends, a feather's touch,
Covering earth, in silence so much.
The pines adorned, with crystal lace,
A frozen dawn, in nature’s embrace.

Time stands still, as dreams unveil,
Through icy paths, we bravely sail.
Echoes whisper, secrets shared,
In winter’s grasp, our hearts laid bare.

With every breath, the cold is sweet,
A journey long, where life and dreams meet.
Through glistening trails, we softly stride,
In the silent beauty, we confide.

And as we roam, the twilight glows,
Amongst the frost, a warmth bestows.
In every heartbeat, hope ignites,
On this silent path, our spirits take flight.

Veil of Ice and Snow

Under the veil, of ice and snow,
Nature whispers, secrets flow.
In a world draped, in purest white,
Magic weaves through day and night.

Frozen branches, glisten bright,
A crystal wonder, pure delight.
Each flake a wish, a story spun,
Under the watch of the winter sun.

With every step, the world transforms,
In the stillness, our hearts reborn.
Veils of silence, cloak the land,
In icy beauty, we take a stand.

As shadows stretch, and whispers fade,
We wander deeper, unafraid.
A journey wrapped, in winter's grace,
In the secret haven, we find our place.

Emerging light, as morning breaks,
Under the veil, the heart awakes.
In the realm of frost, a dance unfolds,
In every breath, a story told.

Beneath a Shimmering Canopy

Beneath the leaves, where sunlight weaves,
A shimmering quilt, that never leaves.
In gentle hues, the shadows play,
As nature's magic lights the way.

Whispers of winds, a lullaby,
Guiding us under the cobalt sky.
In emerald greens and golden light,
We find our paths, our spirits bright.

With every step, the world ignites,
Beneath the canopy, our hearts take flight.
A world alive, in vibrant sound,
In this embrace, pure joy is found.

Moments captured, in golden beams,
Under the dreams that nature dreams.
Together we dance, amidst the trees,
In nature's arms, we find our peace.

As twilight whispers, the day will close,
We gather sweetness, like blooming rose.
In every shimmer, new hope begins,
Beneath the canopy, our journey spins.

Whispers Beneath a Frosty Sky

Whispers dance in the chilly air,
Silent secrets beyond compare.
The moonlight glimmers on snow's white shore,
Nature's breath, a soft welcome door.

Frosted branches sway with grace,
In this tranquil, enchanted space.
Stars twinkle like dreams that have flown,
In the stillness, there's magic shown.

Soft shadows shift as night draws near,
Each flicker of warmth, a heart sincere.
The world sleeps under a silvery shroud,
While dreams gather beneath a midnight cloud.

Whispers of winter gently play,
Embracing the end of the day.
In harmony, the earth breathes slow,
As the frosty winds begin to blow.

Under this vast, celestial dome,
Every heart feels the call of home.
In the quiet, a promise swells,
Of stories that the night gently tells.

Echoes of a Chill Embrace

In the stillness, echoes bloom,
A chill embraces, sweeping gloom.
Frost-kissed air, a gentle sigh,
Whispers linger as hearts comply.

Through the trees, a soft wind weaves,
Carrying tales of autumn leaves.
The world cloaked in a silver hue,
As shadows dance in the evening dew.

With every breath, the silence hums,
Nature's lullaby softly comes.
Stars peek through the fabric of night,
Guiding lost souls with gentle light.

In the dark, a myriad glows,
Songs of the past in the stillness flows.
Underneath this velvet sky,
Whispers call, as time drifts by.

Embracing the chill, we find our way,
Carved in ice, where the memories stay.
In the winter's heart, dreams intertwine,
In the echo of a love divine.

Journey Through the Crystal Veil

A journey calls through a crystal veil,
Where dreams are woven, and whispers sail.
Each step a dance upon the frost,
In this land where the echoes are lost.

Frozen rivers whisper past,
Moments captured, a fleeting blast.
Footprints mark the path we tread,
Through fields of silver, the story spread.

The air is filled with a magic rare,
As starlight glimmers, bright and fair.
Beneath the gaze of a watchful moon,
The heart beats faster, a rhythmic tune.

In silence shared, we find our peace,
Where hopes and fears begin to cease.
The crystal veil, a guide so true,
Reveals the beauty in me and you.

As dawn approaches, shadows flee,
New beginnings call, wild and free.
A journey through this frosty maze,
Leads to warmth in the sun's embrace.

Shadows Cast by the Distant Sun

Shadows stretch as day declines,
Beneath the sun, where nature shines.
Golden hues kiss the fading night,
Creating dreams in fading light.

Gentle winds carry whispers low,
As dusk embraces, the world aglow.
In every corner, soft shadows play,
Painting stories in a surreal way.

Echoes of warmth in the cooling air,
Embracing moments of quiet care.
The horizon blushes, a canvas drawn,
As stars prepare for the coming dawn.

Each flicker of light tells the tale,
Of journeys taken, through the veil.
As the distant sun fades from view,
Shadows linger, embracing the blue.

In the twilight, our hearts take flight,
As shadows weave with the softest light.
In every goodbye, there's a chance to sigh,
Under the gaze of the evening sky.

Frost-kissed Footsteps

Soft crunch beneath my feet,
A world wrapped up in white.
Each step a silent beat,
Guiding me through the night.

Moonlight dances on the ground,
Reflecting dreams once found.
In the hush, a gentle sound,
Nature's whisper all around.

Breath of winter on my skin,
The air is crisp and clear.
Adventures soon begin,
In this landscape, I hold dear.

Footprints lead me on my way,
Stories yet to unfold.
The chill won’t sway my stay,
In a world of purest gold.

Frost-kissed journeys call my name,
Pathways wrapped in dreams.
Each mark, a lasting flame,
In time's soft, flowing streams.

Whispering Pines in White

Pines stand tall, dressed in snow,
Silent sentinels of peace.
Their secrets carried low,
In whispers that never cease.

Branches gleam with crystal grace,
Nature's jewels in the light.
In this enchanted space,
Magic holds the day and night.

Footsteps lead to hidden trails,
Where dreams are born anew.
In the wind, a tale prevails,
Of moments pure and true.

With every breeze that sways,
A melody takes flight.
In the quiet, my heart plays,
To the rhythm of delight.

Whispering pines, sacred ground,
Guardians of all that's bright.
In their arms, I am found,
Lost in the soft moonlight.

Echoes of Snowflakes

Softly falling from the sky,
Each flake a work of art.
They dance in silence, oh so high,
Landing with a gentle heart.

In their descent, stories weave,
Of winters long gone by.
A tapestry that shall deceive,
As they kiss the earth and sigh.

Whirling winds play their song,
While echoes of joy surround.
In the quiet, I belong,
To this magic, tightly bound.

Every flake a unique fate,
Whispering all around.
In this moment, I await,
The beauty that I've found.

Timeless whispers in the cold,
From skies that mirror dreams.
The stillness, a tale retold,
In shimmering frozen beams.

Shadows Beneath the Boughs

In the forest deep and wide,
Shadows linger in the light.
Under boughs where secrets hide,
Mysteries take flight.

Footfalls quiet, heartbeats slow,
Nature's pulse is felt.
In the space where echoes flow,
Ancient magic is dealt.

The branches form a canopy,
Whispering tales of yore.
Beneath this green tapestry,
I wander evermore.

Time unravels in this place,
Moments stretch, then bend.
Each shadow holds a trace,
Of stories without end.

In the stillness, wisdom grows,
Each breath, a timeless quest.
Among the shadows, life bestows,
A chance to simply rest.

Beneath the Ice

Silent whispers hide below,
Chilled secrets deep in snow.
Frozen dreams of life once bred,
Now they slumber, still and dead.

In the depths, the shadows play,
Dancing shapes in shades of gray.
The world above, a frigid place,
In stillness, nature finds its grace.

Crystals gleam in frosty air,
Veils of beauty, stark and rare.
A realm where warmth has lost its fight,
Yet holds a magic, pure and bright.

Echoed breaths of winter's song,
Murmur softly, all night long.
Beneath the ice, a heart beats slow,
Holding stories we don't know.

Awakening when seasons change,
From slumber deep, they rearrange.
Nature's cycle, time's embrace,
Life beneath this cold, white space.

Heartbeats Persist

In silence deep, where shadows dwell,
Life beats on, a gentle swell.
Through the chill, heart rhythms flow,
In the dark, they softly glow.

Each pulse a story, silent song,
Carried where the brave belong.
In each beat, resilience found,
Whispers of life, profound.

Underneath a blanket, white,
Hope springs forth, igniting light.
Though the winter world may freeze,
Life persists upon the breeze.

Echoing through the coldest night,
Faint heartbeats call, a guiding light.
Nature holds them close and tight,
Whispers shared in soft twilight.

In the heart, warmth does reside,
Even when the world has died.
With every breath, we shall insist,
Hearts will fight, for they persist.

Navigating the Frostbitten Expanse

Windswept plains, a frosty trail,
Where dreams are whispered in the gale.
Guided by the moon’s soft glow,
Through the ice and endless snow.

Frostbitten paths stretch near and far,
Twinkling like the northern star.
Footsteps careful, spirits high,
As the snowflakes swirl and fly.

Each breath a cloud, each turn a chance,
Mapping out this frozen dance.
Where shadows hide and echoes call,
Nature’s canvas, vast and tall.

In the stillness, courage grows,
Amidst the chill and biting woes.
With hearts as shields, we venture wide,
Together through the winter’s tide.

Navigating this expanse vast,
Finding strength in every blast.
For in the cold, our souls ignite,
Crafting warmth from the night.

Serenity Wrapped in White

A quiet world in ashen hue,
Tender moments, fresh and new.
Cloaked in peace, the landscape lies,
Cradled gently 'neath winter skies.

Flakes of snow like whispers fall,
Covering the earth, a gentle thrall.
Serenity in every flake,
A tranquil breath, a calm awake.

Stillness reigns, where silence grows,
Nature hums in softest throes.
In this white embrace, we find,
Harmony of heart and mind.

Time moves slow, beneath the frost,
Glimmers of magic, never lost.
In the quiet, hope takes flight,
Wrapped in serenity, pure delight.

With each step, a dance unfolds,
Stories woven, quietly told.
In peace, we wander, hand in hand,
Through this calm, enchanting land.

Echoes from Branches Deep

Among the trees where echoes play,
Whispers linger, soft and gray.
Frozen branches, arms upraised,
Nature's symphony, lovingly phrased.

Cradled by the winter's hush,
In the stillness, hearts will rush.
Songs of old, in silence shared,
Echoes call, reminding, prepared.

Beneath the snow, the roots entwine,
Holding secrets, life’s design.
In heartbeats mixed with nature’s pulse,
Awakening the dormant impulse.

Branches crack as cold winds sigh,
Hearts may ache, yet spirits fly.
Through the frost, the memories seep,
Of warmth and light, from branches deep.

Listen close, to winter’s tune,
In the quiet, find the moon.
Echoes linger, softly bright,
Calling forth the stars tonight.

Crystalline Echoes in Silent Woods

Whispers linger in the air,
Frost-kissed branches, crisp and bare.
Footsteps soft on powdered ground,
Nature's hush, a precious sound.

Sunlight dances through the trees,
Sparkling bright, a gentle breeze.
Shadows play where silence dwells,
In this realm, the magic swells.

Echoes of a distant stream,
Reflect the light, a fleeting dream.
Mossy stones, the quiet throng,
In this peace, I feel so strong.

Every branch a story tells,
In the woods, sweet secrets dwell.
Caught in time, the world stands still,
Beneath the whispers, I feel thrill.

Crystalline echoes softly blend,
In this silence, I transcend.
Warmth of sunlight on my face,
In the woods, I find my place.

The Unfurling of Winter's Embrace

A blanket white covers the ground,
In every corner, peace is found.
Nature sleeps, the world holds still,
In winter's grasp, I find my will.

Glistening frost on every tree,
Winter's charm, a reverie.
Branches bow, heavy with snow,
In this silence, soft winds blow.

Crisp air fills with scents divine,
Breath of winter, crisp and fine.
Softly glows the twilight sky,
As day whispers a sweet goodbye.

Stars awaken, icy and bright,
Painting dreams in the still night.
Every flake a tale to weave,
In winter's heart, I dare believe.

Moments linger, time stands still,
Wrapped in warmth, I feel the thrill.
Winter's embrace, so deep and wide,
In this season, I abide.

Beneath the Veil of Winter's Breath

Beneath the veil of frosty light,
The world transforms, a pure delight.
Each breath forms a tender cloud,
In this magic, I stand proud.

Gentle flakes begin to fall,
Whispered secrets, nature's call.
Cloaked in white, the earth shall sleep,
Winter's promise, dreams to keep.

Frozen streams in silver chains,
Echoes soft of winter rains.
Quietude in every nook,
Time to ponder, time to look.

Candles flicker in the night,
Illuminating soft twilight.
In the silence, shadows play,
Softly guiding me on my way.

Wrapped in warmth of evening's glow,
Beneath the stars, a world in snow.
Winter’s breath a soothing balm,
In this peace, I find my calm.

Seeking Solitude in the Snowfield

Wandering far through fields of white,
Seeking solace, heart takes flight.
Snowflakes dance in the frosty air,
Each one unique, a beauty rare.

Quiet moments stretch like dawn,
In this wilderness, I feel drawn.
With every step, the world recedes,
Nature whispers, my soul feeds.

Mountains loom on either side,
In their shadows, I confide.
Cool winds brush against my face,
In this snowfield, I find grace.

Softly falling, the silence grows,
In the stillness, magic flows.
Every flake a story spun,
Underneath the winter sun.

Seeking peace in the quiet vale,
As I wander, I prevail.
In the snow, my spirit's free,
In solitude, I long to be.

A Gleam of Light on the White Road

A gleam of light on a frosty morn,
Guides weary travelers, tired and worn.
The path ahead shimmers, pure and bright,
As hope awakens in the dawn's soft light.

Footsteps crunch on the frosted ground,
In silence, beauty and peace abound.
A whisper of promise in every breath,
As nature dances with life and death.

Trees stand tall, cloaked in white,
Their branches heavy, a stunning sight.
Birds take flight, a fleeting trace,
In this moment, time finds its grace.

As shadows stretch with the rising sun,
Journey continues, we’re not yet done.
The road ahead glistens with delight,
Every turn reveals a new insight.

With each step taken, dreams ignite,
On this white road, a path so bright.
We'll carry the light like a treasured stone,
In the heart’s quiet, we’re never alone.

The North Wind's Whisper

The north wind whispers through the trees,
A haunting melody carried by the breeze.
It tells of stories, ancient and old,
Of lands far away, of treasure untold.

Icicles glimmer like crystals of glass,
Each sharp edge tells how the moments pass.
The world is hushed in a soft embrace,
As winter's beauty holds its place.

Clouds dance lightly across the sky,
Casting shadows where secrets lie.
The chill wraps close, a familiar friend,
Reminding us how the seasons blend.

In every gust, a secret sigh,
Of distant travels, of dreams that fly.
With each breath drawn, the spirit lifts,
Carried on winds, our hearts it gifts.

So listen closely to the call of the air,
For the north wind's charm is beyond compare.
In whispers, it teaches the tales of the night,
And fills our thoughts with wondrous light.

Nature's Brilliant Chill

Nature's chill glistens with frost,
In her embrace, no moment’s lost.
Every breath is a plume of white,
A reminder of magic, warm and bright.

The river flows, a crystal sheet,
Where life sleeps softly beneath its feet.
Mountains tower, majestic and bold,
Guardians of wonders, their stories told.

With every step, a crunch, a sigh,
Beneath the vast and endless sky.
The world transformed, a canvas pure,
In nature’s chill, we find the cure.

Frosted fields in morning's dream,
Sparkle and shimmer, a radiant gleam.
As the sun rises, warmth creeps in,
Nature awakens, life begins.

In this season of vibrant hue,
We gather strength, as we start anew.
For in the chill, a promise we find,
A whisper of spring, of love combined.

Frosted Leaves and Silent Dreams

Frosted leaves shimmer under the moon,
Each one a story, a silent tune.
Whispers of seasons that come and go,
In the stillness, the heartbeats flow.

Night descends with a tender touch,
The world in slumber, it means so much.
Each star above, a watchful eye,
Guiding the dreams that softly lie.

In twilight's glow, hopes gently stir,
A dance of shadows, a soothing purr.
The air is crisp, with scents so sweet,
Nature's embrace, where all hearts meet.

Frosty whispers weave through the night,
Caressing the earth in gentle light.
Every leaf, a memory held tight,
Sharing secrets in the hush of night.

With dawn's approach, the veil will lift,
Awakening dreams, nature’s gift.
In each frosted leaf, a tale it seems,
Of silent beauty and cherished dreams.

Lost in the Haze of a Snowstorm

Whispers echo through the white,
A shroud of silence, day to night.
Soft flakes dance, a ghostly waltz,
Lost in dreams, as vision halts.

Rushing winds moan a chilling tune,
Blanket the earth, a quiet rune.
Footprints vanish, trails obscured,
In this maze, we feel assured.

Branches bow beneath the weight,
Nature's beauty, still, sedate.
Shapes emerge, then fade away,
In the storm's embrace, we stay.

Hearts entwined in winter's arms,
Drawn to the peace of hidden charms.
Each flake unique, a wondrous sign,
In the haze, your hand in mine.

As the world melts into peace,
Whispers of love will never cease.
Through the storm, we'll find our way,
Lost in the haze, we'll always stay.

A Footprint's Story in Frozen Time

One single print upon the snow,
Tells a tale we'll come to know.
A journey starts beneath the stars,
Leaving whispers, near and far.

Each stride marks a path anew,
In the cold, a warmth breaks through.
Moments captured, secrets thrum,
Where the heart and silence hum.

Frosty nights, the story grows,
Echoes linger, life bestows.
Through the frost, footprints entwine,
A dance of fate across the line.

Nature's canvas, blank and wide,
Treads reveal where dreams abide.
Every step, a memory spent,
Frozen time, where hearts lament.

A tale within each icy trace,
Yearning echoes in this space.
Though the winter takes its toll,
The footprints speak, they warm the soul.

The Language of Frozen Crystals

Delicate forms, in silence gleam,
Whispers of winter, secrets teem.
Crystals speak in icy tongues,
A language old, where beauty clungs.

Each flake a word, a tale unfolds,
Stories of warmth in the bitter cold.
Patterns weave, a tapestry rare,
In frozen art, we glimpse, we stare.

Winter's breath, a soft caress,
Nature's script we must confess.
A dialogue of light and shade,
In every frost, memories made.

The silence sings, a tranquil chime,
Unraveling echoes of lost time.
Crystal voices in the night,
Guide us through with shimmering light.

As the world shimmers, hushes low,
In this quiet, we come to know.
The language whispers, soft and sweet,
In frozen crystals, hearts will meet.

A Trail of Frost and Folklore

In the woods, the stories twine,
A trail of frost, old as time.
Legends dance on glimmered ground,
In every shadow, truths are found.

Old trees whisper tales untold,
Of lost loves and heartbeats bold.
Frosty air carries the lore,
In the silence, we seek more.

The path is etched, each step a song,
A place where dreams and tales belong.
The stars bear witness to our quest,
As whispers lead, we feel their zest.

Every turn, a secret waits,
In the frost, enchanted fates.
Folklore rests upon the leaves,
Echoes of those who believed.

With every footprint pressed so slight,
We walk the line of dark and light.
In the frost, our hearts will soar,
On this trail of frost and lore.

A Delicate Dance on Icy Trails

With every step, the ice will gleam,
A fragile world, a frozen dream.
The whispers of the cold winds call,
As nature dons her crystal shawl.

Footprints trace a fleeting grace,
In this enchanting, frosty space.
The pine trees sway, their boughs align,
A quiet dance, so pure, divine.

Sunrise paints the snow with light,
Transforming shadows into bright.
A tapestry of white unfolds,
Each moment precious, each one holds.

Laughter spills like melting streams,
In the heart, we keep our dreams.
Through icy trails, our spirits soar,
A timeless dance, forevermore.

Frost-kissed Memories Beneath Oak

Beneath the oak, where shadows play,
Frost-kissed memories softly sway.
The crunch of leaves, a whispered sound,
In twilight's glow, our hearts are found.

Winter's breath paints branches white,
As stars emerge to greet the night.
The air is crisp, the world stands still,
Amongst the oaks, we find our thrill.

Footsteps echo on frosty ground,
In every silence, love is found.
Golden hues of twilight fade,
A treasure trove of memories made.

Against the bark, our names inscribed,
In winter's clasp, our hearts imbibed.
Each moment shared, forever true,
Beneath the oak, me and you.

Veils of Mist Over Glacial Waters

Veils of mist, a soft embrace,
Glacial waters, a tranquil space.
The stillness holds a secret song,
In nature's realm, where we belong.

Reflections dance on icy streams,
Shimmering whispers of our dreams.
The mountains guard their snowy crowns,
While time drapes silk in gentle gowns.

Crystalline droplets slowly fall,
A symphony, the world's soft call.
Underneath the mist, life thrives,
In every breath, the spirit dives.

Tranquil heart, and breath so deep,
In this hush, the world we keep.
Veils of mist and glacial light,
Guide us gently, through the night.

Frosted Ferns and Winter Dreams

Frosted ferns beneath the snow,
Whispers of winter, soft and low.
Each frond adorned with icy lace,
Nature's artwork, a tranquil grace.

In the quiet, dreams take flight,
Gliding gently through the night.
A world reborn in white and gray,
Where hopes arise, come what may.

Echoes linger in the air,
Every moment, rich and rare.
With heartbeats sync'd in harmony,
We weave our tales, you and me.

Frosted ferns, and memories gleam,
In this chilly, beautiful dream.
Winter's kiss, a kind embrace,
As we find joy in every place.

Frosted Branches

Beneath the weight of icy glaze,
The branches droop in winter's daze.
A shimmer caught in pale moonlight,
They whisper secrets of the night.

Each twig adorned with crystal tears,
A story woven through the years.
The cold wind sings a haunting tune,
As stars peek out, a silver boon.

Through silent nights, the world stands still,
With every breath, a frozen thrill.
Nature rests, her beauty pure,
In frosted dreams, we find allure.

Soft snowflakes kiss the sleeping ground,
A quiet magic all around.
In this embrace of wintery air,
Frosted branches stand with grace.

As dawn unfolds, a gentle hue,
The world awakens fresh and new.
With every light, the glimmers fade,
But memories of frost will stay made.

Lidded Dreams

Beneath the lid of slumber deep,
In twilight's grasp, the dreamers leap.
With visions bright, they soar and glide,
Across the sea of stars, they ride.

Each whisper soft, a tale untold,
In realms of magic, brave and bold.
They wander where the shadows play,
In dreams, reality's kept at bay.

Through misty halls, the echoes ring,
Of fleeting joy, of winter's spring.
Lidded dreams, a soft embrace,
In every heart, a sacred space.

As dawn's first light begins to creep,
The dreamers wake from gentle sleep.
Yet in their hearts, those visions gleam,
A treasure held in every dream.

With every night, the cycle spins,
Awake or asleep, the journey begins.
In lidded dreams, we find our place,
United in this timeless grace.

Echoes of a Snowy Silence

In the hush of ashen skies,
A world wrapped tight, a soft disguise.
The flakes descend, a delicate dance,
Each whisper holds a fleeting chance.

Footsteps muffled beneath the white,
In snowy silence, hearts take flight.
So still, the air a tender shroud,
With echoes lost in dreams allowed.

A blanket weaves the earth anew,
Transforming all that we once knew.
Through chilly dreams, in frosted breath,
The silence sings a song of depth.

As twilight falls, the shadows blend,
The snowy whispers gently mend.
In every flake, a story spun,
Of winter nights and setting sun.

Embrace the quiet, feel its grace,
In echoes soft, we find our place.
For in the stillness, hearts collide,
In snowy silence, dreams abide.

A Tundra Serenade

In the tundra, vast and wide,
A serenade of nature's pride.
With whispers from the icy breeze,
It tells a tale beneath the trees.

The ground adorned with frosted lace,
Each crystal glint, a fleeting trace.
With every note of winter's call,
The tundra sings, enchanting all.

Through valleys deep, and mountains tall,
The serenade weaves through the sprawl.
It dances with the northern lights,
A symphony of starry nights.

As shadows stretch and daylight fades,
The musical notes in silence wade.
For in this land of frost and chill,
The tundra's song forever will.

A melody of peace unfolds,
A magic found in heartbeats bold.
So listen close, let spirits rise,
In tundra's grace, our hearts comply.

Enchanted in Crystal Layers

Enchanted woodlands draped in frost,
In crystal layers, a beauty crossed.
Each branch aglow with nature's hand,
A shimmering lace across the land.

The whispers of the winter trees,
As gentle as the frozen breeze.
Beneath the weight of winter's sigh,
The world transforms beneath the sky.

As sunbeams dance on icy crowns,
The landscape glimmers, nature's gowns.
With every step, the echoes ring,
In crystal dreams, the heart takes wing.

In silence wrapped, a peaceful night,
The stars above, a twinkling sight.
Enchanted dreams await the dawn,
In frosted realms, we carry on.

Let spirit roam in gentle glee,
Through layers of crystal, wild and free.
In winter's charm, we find the way,
To warm our hearts as night meets day.

Where Silence Reigns in Winter's Hold

In the stillness, whispers freeze,
A world wrapped tight in icy breath.
Footsteps muffled by the trees,
Nature holds her heart in depth.

Boughs adorned with crystal light,
Embers of a sunlight's past.
The moon's soft glow, a tender sight,
Each moment, fleeting, yet vast.

Frosted air, a quiet sigh,
Stars twinkle in the endless night.
The world beneath a soft blanket lies,
Where silence reigns, all feels right.

Winds carry tales of old,
Frozen echoes softly call.
In the grip of winter’s hold,
Time seems to halt, as shadows fall.

Yet in this chill, a warmth remains,
The hearth's glow, a flickering light.
Memories linger in our veins,
In winter’s silence, love takes flight.

A Journey Along a Glacial Whistle

Amidst the mountains high and bold,
A glacial whisper calls my name.
Through icy paths and stories told,
Nature beckons, never the same.

Footprints trace the snowy scene,
In a dance with the ancient ice.
With every step, the world is keen,
In the depths, I pay the price.

The winds carry tales through the pines,
Secrets held in chilling breath.
Each moment lost in frozen lines,
A journey marked by life and death.

Echoes of laughter, faint yet clear,
As I wander through time and space.
With every heartbeat, the end draws near,
Yet hope lingers in this place.

So follow the whistle, wild and free,
Embrace the chill that winds around.
Each glacial note sings of mystery,
On this journey, life is found.

Memories Fading Like Snowflakes

Once vibrant dreams danced in the sun,
Now they drift like flakes in flight.
Each a story, each a run,
Fading softly into night.

In the warm glow of forgotten days,
I chase the echoes of my past.
But like the snow, time slips away,
Leaving traces that cannot last.

Faces blur in the winter breeze,
Familiar laughter now so faint.
Yet in the chill, a heart can freeze,
Remembering the joy, the paint.

Like snowflakes lost in the vast expanse,
Memories glisten, then dissolve.
In silence, they perform their dance,
A fleeting moment to resolve.

Embrace the cold, the fading light,
Hold dear what warmth you can retain.
For like the snowflakes in their flight,
So too are memories, joy and pain.

The Dance of Shadows and Frost

Underneath the pale moon's glow,
Shadows waltz upon the ground.
Frosty tendrils start to flow,
In whispered silence, they are found.

Branches sway in a gentle breeze,
Each movement casts a fleeting charm.
Nature’s rhythm brings me to my knees,
In this embrace, I find my calm.

Every flake, a haunting trace,
Falling softly through the night.
In the dark, I find my place,
A dance of shadows, pure delight.

As the frost paints the world anew,
Magic whispers in every crevice.
In this dance, the night feels true,
Where silence reigns, no need for preface.

So let us sway beneath the stars,
With shadows twirling all around.
In winter’s grip, we’ll conquer scars,
In the dance of frost, we are unbound.

Frosted Memories on the Trail

Upon the path where shadows play,
Footprints linger, fading away.
Whispers of laughter, soft and clear,
Echoes of moments we hold dear.

Beneath the trees with branches gray,
Winter's breath sings a gentle sway.
Every flake a story told,
Wrapped in warmth against the cold.

The bitter chill, a fleeting kiss,
Memories tangled in winter's bliss.
A heart once heavy, now light as air,
Frosted dreams weaving everywhere.

As daylight wanes, the twilight sighs,
Painting the world in pale sunrise.
We'll chase the frost with mugs of cheer,
Collect our dreams, hold them near.

In every step, the past remains,
Frosted memories, love's sweet chains.
On this trail where we've walked long,
We find our peace, forever strong.

Snowbound Soliloquy

Alone I sit, the world a blur,
Snowflakes dance, their soft demur.
Whispers of winter wrap me tight,
In this cocoon, I'll find my light.

The window glows with silver grace,
Each flake falls in gentle embrace.
Thoughts drift like clouds in the sky,
While time stands still as moments fly.

Silent echoes in a frozen breath,
Life's sweet promises echo like death.
Yet here I breathe the cold air deep,
In dreams awakened, I shall leap.

The world beyond, a pristine sheet,
Blanketing life where past and present meet.
With every breath, the solitude grows,
In the heart of snow, the silence flows.

As night unfolds, stars start to gleam,
In snowbound dreams, I weave my theme.
With whispers soft, the moon shall know,
The stories that blossom in winter's snow.

Chilling Winds and Warm Souls

Blustering winds cut through the night,
Yet hearts aglow, feeling so right.
In the chill, we find our grace,
Warmth ignites in this sacred space.

Together we'll wander where ice meets flame,
Every glance holds a whispered name.
Through frosted air, with laughter bold,
We weave a tapestry of silver and gold.

Branches crackle, the forest sighs,
Chilling winds push the clouds on high.
But in this moment, hand in hand,
Together we'll make our timeless stand.

Embers glow beneath a starlit dome,
In winter's heart, we've found our home.
With every gust, love's spirit whirls,
In chilling winds, we unfurl.

So let them blow, let them scream and howl,
In warmth we'll gather, heart and soul.
Through winter's grasp, we'll always stay,
Chilling winds can't lead us astray.

Twinkle of Stars on Frozen Nights

In frozen stillness, stars ignite,
Twinkling softly, a celestial sight.
They whisper secrets of ancient tales,
In the midnight air, where wonder prevails.

Beneath the moon, the world asleep,
Dreams take flight, in silence deep.
Every sparkle, a wish sent high,
On frozen nights, we learn to fly.

The crisp air hums with a magic glow,
Guiding our hearts through the winter's flow.
Each breath we take, a story ends,
In the tapestry where stars are friends.

As shadows dance on frosty ground,
In the stillness, our hopes are found.
The night embraces, with arms so wide,
In twinkle of stars, we take our ride.

So watch the sky, let your spirit roam,
In the cold embrace, we'll find our home.
For on these nights, as dreams take flight,
Stars whisper love, in frozen light.

The Hush of a Frosty Night

Snowflakes drift in silent flight,
Beneath the stars, the world feels right.
A blanket white on slumbering land,
Whispers echo, soft and grand.

Trees stand tall, their branches bare,
Wrapped in frost, they breathe the air.
The moon casts glow, a silver sheen,
In this stillness, all is serene.

Footsteps muffled, hearts take pause,
Nature's breath, a whispered cause.
Time slows down, the night invites,
Enfolded by the frosty sights.

Creatures nest, a cozy stay,
Dreams weave warm in winter's play.
Stars twinkle in the icy dome,
Guiding wanderers, far from home.

As night deepens, shadows shift,
In the hush, sweet moments lift.
Wrapped in blankets of soft snow,
The world at peace, a gentle glow.

A Tapestry of Glacial Hues

Icicles dangle, sharp and bright,
Reflecting colors, pure delight.
A canvas painted cold and clear,
Each hue whispers winter's cheer.

Mountains rise with peaks of glass,
Captured light in moments pass.
The sky a canvas, blue and gray,
Where sunlight dances, bold and gay.

Frozen rivers glide and weave,
In the stillness, hearts believe.
Nature's art, a masterpiece,
In chilly breath, we find our peace.

Wind sings softly through the trees,
A lullaby in icy breeze.
Each branch holds stories, time unfurled,
A tapestry woven in winter's world.

Colors blend in twilight's glow,
A warm embrace in winter's snow.
Beneath the stars that brightly shone,
A glacial scene to call our own.

Lullabies in the Land of Snow

In the air, a gentle sigh,
Winter sings a lullaby.
Softly falling, flakes descend,
Nature's song, the heart's best friend.

Blankets cover earth in white,
Cradled close, the world feels right.
Each flake spins a tale anew,
Whispers sweet, both soft and true.

Children laugh, their spirits bright,
Building dreams in purest white.
Snowmen stand with button eyes,
Underneath the winter skies.

Candles flicker, shadows dance,
Fires crackle, hearts in trance.
Together here, we find our place,
In the land of snow, a warm embrace.

When darkness falls, the stars awake,
Guiding dreams that we can make.
Lullabies, in whispers flow,
Carrying wishes in the snow.

Threads of Silver on the Frozen Ground

Beneath the frost, a whisper stirs,
Nature’s lace, as silence purrs.
Threads of silver, glistening bright,
A canvas woven, pure delight.

Morning breaks, and shadows play,
Across the fields where snowflakes lay.
Nature spins her fine attire,
Each thread a story, heart's desire.

Footprints traced in icy art,
Map the journeys from the heart.
Through winter's veil, we find our way,
With threads of silver holding sway.

Crisp air fills our lungs with cheer,
In the stillness, we draw near.
Together, wrapped in nature's quilt,
Life awakens, softly built.

As twilight falls, the world aglow,
Underneath the silver snow.
We weave our dreams, with every sound,
In this magic, warmth is found.

Touch of Frost on Worn Boots

Beneath the chill of morning light,
Old boots crunch silently in white.
Whispers of winter softly call,
Each step a dance, a gentle thrall.

Frosted edges brush the ground,
Nature's breath is all around.
A quiet world, a hidden grace,
In this moment, time finds place.

Air so crisp, it bites and stings,
Echoes of the season's wings.
Worn paths lead to memories deep,
Where dreams are sown and secrets keep.

Colors fade in the morning glow,
Footprints tell the tales we know.
Through whispers of the frozen air,
We gather warmth, a moment rare.

As sunlight breaks, the frost will fade,
But in our hearts, the chill is stayed.
Forever tied to winter's song,
In worn boots, we still belong.

Carved Paths in the Snow

In the hush of falling snow,
Footsteps linger, soft and slow.
Each mark a story, life's embrace,
Carved connections in this space.

Branches bowed with frosty crowns,
Nature dresses in winter gowns.
The silent woods, a canvas pure,
Where hearts find peace, and thoughts endure.

Beneath a sky of silver sheen,
The world feels fresh, the air pristine.
Paths entwined, we wander far,
Guided by a hidden star.

Beyond the pines, a glimmer lies,
As sunlight breaks through cloudy skies.
With every step, new dreams we sow,
In these carved paths, our spirits grow.

Lost in beauty, we drift and roam,
Finding solace, feeling home.
Each footfall whispers tales of yore,
In winter's grip, we can explore.

Solitude Amongst the Evergreens

In stillness wrapped by the tall pines,
Where shadows play and sunlight shines.
Solitude dances in the breeze,
Whispers soft among the leaves.

A peaceful heart, a quiet mind,
In nature's arms, we seek to find.
Moments linger, time suspended,
Amongst the green, our fears are mended.

Lonely trails where thoughts can roam,
Every inch a glimpse of home.
Branches sway to a silent tune,
Underneath the watchful moon.

Life unfolds in layers slow,
Hidden secrets in the snow.
Amongst the evergreens, we stand,
Hand in hand with this vast land.

As twilight blooms, the stars ignite,
Filling the dark with tiny light.
In solitude, we find our way,
With every breath, we welcome day.

Glimmering Frost on the Horizon

As dawn awakens the sleeping night,
A glimmer shines, so pure and bright.
Frosty jewels adorn the scene,
Nature's canvas, crisp and clean.

Mountains bow beneath the glow,
Soft whispers of the winds that blow.
Colors merge in a frozen dance,
Inviting all to take a chance.

Horizons painted with gentle hues,
A world transformed, a life renewed.
Every breath, a shimmering sigh,
Underneath the expansive sky.

In this moment, time stands still,
Life’s hidden wonders, hearts we fill.
As sunlight kisses frosted ground,
A symphony of peace is found.

In the distance, dreams arise,
As glowing frost meets waking skies.
With every dawn, new hopes are spun,
In the glimmering light, we run.

www.ingramcontent.com/pod-product-compliance
Ingram Content Group UK Ltd.
Pitfield, Milton Keynes, MK11 3LW, UK
UKHW031956131224
452403UK00010B/507

9 789916 793558